★ SPORTS STARS ★

LISA LESLIE
QUEEN OF THE COURT

BY MARK STEWART

SCHOLASTIC INC.

New York Toronto London Auckland Sydney
Mexico City New Delhi Hong Kong Buenos Aires

Photo Credits

☆ CONTENTS ☆

GIVE THE BALL TO LISA

Lisa Leslie waits patiently. She's the 6' 5"
center for the Los Angeles Sparks. Her team
is setting up their offense. The Sparks are a team
in the Women's National Basketball Association,
or WNBA. Lisa is their best player.

Lisa's teammate dribbles. She prepares to pass.
Lisa is in the foul lane. She uses her strength to
get free. Her teammate sees her. She slips the ball
to Lisa.

Lisa spins around gracefully. She banks the
ball off the glass. It goes in. She scores. But she
doesn't celebrate. Instead, she rushes downcourt
to play defense. She tries to steal the ball from
the other team. She tries to keep the opponent from
shooting. If they do shoot, she rebounds.

Lisa first began playing basketball when she was in middle school. She has been an amazing player ever since. In high school, she was the top female player in the country. With her help, the U.S. women's basketball team won two Olympic gold medals. She has led the Sparks to two WNBA titles.

Lisa joined the WNBA in 1997. Since then, she has worked hard for the league and for her team. She has helped make both successful. She has inspired tons of WNBA fans. Many girls dream of playing basketball like Lisa Leslie. But it almost didn't turn out that way.

★ 2 ★

GROWING UP

Lisa Leslie was just four years old when she learned terrible news. Her father was no longer a part of the family. He had walked out on Lisa and her sisters. Lisa saw him only once over the next eight years. From time to time, he helped out with a few dollars. Then, when Lisa was twelve, he died. Now the Leslies were completely on their own.

Lisa's mother took action. Christine Leslie knew she needed a good job to support her girls, so she scraped up the money to buy an eighteen-wheel tractor trailer. She became a trucker.

Lisa (right) poses with her mom and two sisters in their eighteen-wheel truck.

Unfortunately, truckers have to spend long hours on the road. This meant that Christine was away from home a lot. She had to hire someone to watch the girls. "There were some sad times," Lisa remembers. "Mom had to travel so far and so long. But we understood she had to do it. It made me mature really fast. I had so much to do."

✶ ✶ ✶

Lisa missed her mother a lot. She looked forward
to the summers. That's when she and her sister
traveled with their mom on the road. To save
money, they slept on a narrow bed in the back of
the truck's cab. It would have been a tight squeeze
for anyone. But it was especially true for Lisa.
By seventh grade, she was already six feet tall.

Back then, Lisa's height attracted a lot of
attention. People always asked her if she played
basketball. She played a little. But always having
to answer the same question annoyed her. As a
result, she began to hate
basketball. She wanted to
give up the game. But
her friend Sharon Hargrove
wouldn't let her.

**Lisa practices her
dribbling skills.**

★ ★ ★

Sharon was a great basketball player. She talked Lisa into trying out for the junior high school team. Surprise! Lisa discovered that she really enjoyed the game! "I played center for the first time," she recalls. "Our team went 7–0. I just changed my whole attitude. I guess it was my destiny. But I never knew it."

Lisa quickly learned to use her height. It helped her beat smaller players. But she knew that her size alone was not enough. She needed more to become a great player. So she began working on her basketball skills. Her cousin Craig helped her. They worked hard.

Lisa wanted to be a great scorer and a tough defender. She also wanted to become really strong. So she and Craig worked on her shooting. She also did lots of push-ups and sit-ups. And she spent a lot of time playing on playground courts. That's where the best players in her neighborhood were. She wanted to be as good as they were.

Lisa learned to shoot from all parts of the court.

Lisa wanted to play like her favorite player. That was James Worthy of the Los Angeles Lakers. "I loved to watch James because he was a go-to player," she says. "Whenever the Lakers needed a basket in a big game, they would

Lisa's favorite player was James Worthy of the Los Angeles Lakers.

give it to 'Big Game James.'" Lisa wanted to be like that. She wanted to come through when her team needed a basket. She wanted to be a go-to player.

By the time Lisa got to high school, she was very tall. She stood over 6' 2". She made the varsity basketball team. She started every game. That was unusual for a freshman. Two years later, she had become one of the best players in Los Angeles.

Lisa's basketball success made her mother proud. But Lisa's grades made her even prouder. Lisa was a straight-A student. She also played volleyball and was on the track team, and that wasn't even enough to keep her busy. She was also voted class president in the 10th, 11th, and 12th grades!

When Lisa started her senior season, she was 6' 5". Every college wanted her to play for them.

She was a great shooter. Most tall players weren't. That made her special. Colleges knew she would be great.

In high school, Lisa became a star on the Morningside Lady Monarchs basketball team.

★ ★ ★

Her high school team just kept winning. Often, they were way ahead at the end of the first half. When that happened, the coach would pull Lisa out for the second half. That way, other teammates got a chance to play. Still, Lisa averaged over 27 points and 15 rebounds a game, and she usually blocked five to ten shots as well.

Finally, the end of the season came. It was Lisa's last high school game. And what an incredible game it was! Lisa was trying to break her school's scoring record. Her teammates kept giving her the ball. Lisa kept scoring. In the first quarter, she scored 49 points. In the second quarter, she scored 52 more. By halftime, Lisa's team was up 102–24! Forget the school scoring record! Lisa needed just five more points to break the national scoring record!

Lisa ruled over most other players. Here the scoreboard shows that the score is already 83–31.

However, the other team was unhappy. They didn't like losing so badly. In the locker room they took a vote. They decided to forfeit, or give up, the game. Their coach came out and told the referees. "That was probably the highlight of my career," Lisa says. "I just started making all of these baskets. The other team just decided not to come out to finish the game."

It seemed unfair that Lisa would lose her chance to make history. The referees agreed. They awarded Lisa's team four technical fouls. Lisa stepped to the line. This was her chance. She made all four! But later, the points were taken away. Officials said that the other team had already forfeited. That meant the game was over. Lisa shouldn't have shot the fouls.

Still, Lisa scored 101 points in the game. And that was only during the first half! But some people didn't like what Lisa had done. Some coaches, fans, and writers claimed that she was a bad sport. They said she played too hard against weaker, smaller teams.

Lisa took all of this in stride. She was sorry that she had made the other team look bad. But for her, it was all about basketball. As she says, "It wasn't personal. They knew I was going for the record. I thought knowing that would take

some of the hurt away from being beaten so badly. I wasn't trying to rub anyone's nose in the dirt. I was only trying for the record."

Though she's now a pro, Lisa is still amazed by her last high school game.

★ 3 ★

COLLEGE YEARS

Lisa Leslie could have gone to any college in the country. But she decided to go to the University of Southern California. She wanted to stay close to home. She could hardly wait to play college ball. She was careful not to seem cocky. But deep down she believed that she could become the top player in the country.

After her first college game, lots of other people began to think the same thing. In that game, Lisa's team played the University of Texas. Lisa scored 30 points. She got 20 rebounds. She stole the ball twice. And she blocked two shots. Lisa's team won, 88–77. That was just the beginning. The season got better from there. Lisa finished the season as the top freshman scorer and rebounder.

Lisa stretches before a game.

Lisa is one of the few female basketball players who can dunk.

★ ★ ★

That summer, Lisa made a special trip. She traveled to England as a member of the U.S. women's team. They were playing at the World University Games. No one could take their eyes off the talented young center. And no one could have guessed the surprise Lisa had for the crowd. She made a big slam dunk. It was right before her team's game against Spain. Fans went wild. Then Lisa and the team beat Spain for the gold.

Lisa had been able to dunk since the ninth grade. But she didn't do it during games. It was too dangerous. Says Lisa, "It's more dangerous for women. That's because other women aren't used to being dunked on. So sometimes they accidentally undercut you."

★ ★ ★

It didn't seem like Lisa could get any better. But she knew she could. She was a great player. But she had her weak spots. She wanted to become a better defender. And she wanted to play closer to the basket. She worked hard. And the practice paid off. Lisa's shooting got much better during her second season. She also blocked the ball more.

That year, Lisa became a second team All-American. She also became a semifinalist for the Naismith Player of the Year award. Lisa was thrilled by these honors. She vowed to work even harder and play even better.

Then came Lisa's junior year. She was still playing well. She broke the school record for blocked shots. Everyone thought she was amazing. Surely she couldn't get any better.

Lisa (right) fights for a better position under the basket.

Lisa's great shooting made her third on her college's all-time scoring list.

But she did. As a senior she truly came into her own. She saved her best efforts for big games. In these games, Lisa racked up the points. She also pulled down a lot of rebounds.

Her team went all the way to the NCAA quarterfinals. There, they lost to Louisiana Tech. That ended Lisa's amazing college career. She was third on her college's all-time scoring list. She was fourth in rebounding. She was first in blocked shots. She was a very impressive player. Lisa was the nation's player of the year. The vote was unanimous. That means that everyone voted for Lisa!

★ 4 ★

GOLD-MEDAL PERFORMANCE

L isa Leslie's basketball travels were just beginning. After her incredible senior year, she went to Atlanta. There she joined the U.S. team for the Goodwill Games. She was the best player on the court. She averaged 19 points per game. She hit most of her shots. Her play helped the U.S. team win the gold medal.

From there, Lisa went to Italy. She joined the Italian women's professional league. Instantly, she became a star. At the time, there were no pro teams in the United States. So Lisa had to go overseas to play pro ball. But it wasn't what she really wanted. What she wanted was to play pro ball at home.

★ ★ ★

In 1995, Lisa tried out for the women's Olympic basketball team. The team would play for the gold at the 1996 Olympics. In 1992, Lisa had been the youngest player at the Olympic trials. She was one of the last players cut. Since then, it had been her dream to play in the Olympics. Now was her chance.

"I was so excited," Lisa remembers. "There were about 56 women trying out for the team. It got cut down to 20. I was one of them. Then we each had to go into a room where they would tell you if you made it. I went in. They said, 'Lisa, congratulations.' I just shouted 'Yeah!'"

Tara VanDerveer was the U.S. Olympic coach.

Lisa made many close friends on the Olympic team.

★ ★ ★

The Olympic coach had a plan for winning the gold. She would take her team on a world tour. They would spend over a year traveling. They would play a lot of teams in other countries. They would get experience. They would learn to work together. It was a long time to be on the road. But Lisa was ready for it.

There were 14 months before the Olympics. Lisa and her teammates hit the road. They traveled over 102,245 miles! They found themselves on courts in Russia, China, and Australia. They played some great teams.

Often, the games were very difficult. Yet Lisa's team always came out on top. When they finished the tour, their record was 52–0. They hadn't lost once! The players had really come together. Lisa says it was one of the closest teams she has ever been on.

The summer of 1996 arrived. The Olympic Games were beginning. Lisa's team was the toast of the sports world. Everyone was watching them. How would they do? They were great. But the team's past hung like a shadow over them.

At the last Olympics, the American women had lost badly. Then they had been beaten by Brazil at the World Championships. So now they wanted to win. There were tough teams from China and Australia to beat. Winning wouldn't be easy. They were the home team. The pressure was on. They had to play well.

Lisa grabs a rebound against Australia.

Lisa battles for the ball against Ukraine's Lyudmila Nazarenko.

The U.S. team was determined to win the gold medal.

And play well they did. It started with the opening tip of the first game. Lisa and her teammates were just incredible. They won their first five games easily. Lisa made it known that she was the main inside threat. She ruled the court during games against Cuba, Australia, and other countries. Lisa even scored 35 points against Japan. That was the most ever scored by an American woman in the Olympics!

★ ★ ★

Then came the gold medal game against Brazil. The coach wanted Lisa to do something different. She asked Lisa to play farther away from the basket. The idea was to draw the Brazilian center away from the basket as well. That would open up the lane. Lisa's team could make quick cuts and easy follow-up shots. The plan worked on offense. But it didn't work on defense. Lisa was getting beaten. Suddenly, the coach pulled Lisa from the game!

It turned out to be the wake-up call Lisa needed. When she returned to the game, Lisa ruled both ends of the court. She made 12 of 14 shots. She scored 29 points. Her team won, 111–87. They had played a lot of games. They had traveled many miles. And finally, they had played their very best when it counted the most. They had scored more points than any team in Olympic history.

At first, Lisa struggled against Brazil.

Lisa and her teammates
celebrate their victory
over Brazil.

Lisa and her teammates were holding hands and crying when they got their gold medals. They knew how important their win was. It was not just for themselves or their country. It was also for the sport of women's basketball. "It was just very emotional for me," Lisa remembers.

The U.S. team members receive their gold medals.

★ 5 ★

A PRO STAR

L isa didn't stop after winning a gold medal. She has continued to make history. She helped the U.S. women's team win another gold medal at the 2000 Olympics. Two years later, she helped them win again at the U.S. World Championships. For her performance she was named Most Valuable Player. When the WNBA started, Lisa really wanted it to succeed. Playing pro ball at home had been one of her dreams. She worked hard to help make the WNBA a success.

Lisa's team, the Sparks, is one of the best in the league. They won WNBA titles in 2001 and 2002. In 2002, Lisa was named Most Valuable Player of the WNBA Championship. She was also named Most Valuable Player of the All-Star Game.

Lisa's first gold medal was just the beginning.

Lisa receives a kiss from Mom after being drafted by the Sparks.

LESLIE 1

Lisa made a historic slam dunk in 2002.

But the year before was even more amazing. Lisa was named Most Valuable Player of the regular season, the championship, and the All-Star Game! She was the first player ever to get all three awards in one season. Wow!

Lisa did something else amazing in 2002. She dunked the ball during a game. It was against the Miami Sol. Lisa was the first WNBA player ever to dunk in a game.

Lisa knows that girls who play basketball look up to her. Says Lisa, "Ten or fifteen years from now, you will hear girls saying who their favorite players were. It'll probably be one of us."

Lisa hopes to inspire young girls who want to play pro ball.

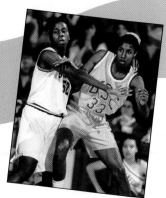

C ★ H ★ R ★ O ★ N

1972	• Lisa is born on July 7th.
1989	• Lisa leads the U.S.A. Junior World Championship team in scoring and rebounding.
1990	• Lisa scores 101 points in a half during the last game of her senior year.
1991	• Lisa finishes her first season at the University of Southern California. She is named national NCAA Freshman of the Year and PAC-10 Freshman of the Year.
1992	• Lisa earns All-American honors for the first time.
1993	• Lisa is named U.S.A. Basketball Female Athlete of the Year and College Player of the Year.
1994–95	• Lisa travels to Italy to play professional basketball.
1995	• Lisa makes the U.S. Olympic women's basketball team. The team goes on a 52-game world tour.

O ⋆ L ⋆ O ⋆ G ⋆ Y

1996 • Lisa leads the Olympic team to a gold medal in Atlanta, Georgia.

1997 • Lisa joins the Los Angeles Sparks of the WNBA. That year, she leads the WNBA in rebounds.

2000 • Lisa wins another gold medal with the U.S. team at the 2000 Olympics in Sydney, Australia.

2001 • Lisa wins the regular season, All-Star Game, and Championship MVP awards. She leads the Sparks to a WNBA title.

2002 • Lisa leads the Sparks to another title. She wins the All-Star Game and Championship MVP awards. She helps the U.S. team win a gold medal at the U.S.A. World Championships. She becomes the first WNBA player to dunk in a game.

LISA LESLIE

Name **Lisa Leslie**
Born **July 7, 1972**
Height **6' 5"**
Weight **170 pounds**
College **University of Southern California**
Pro Team **Los Angeles Sparks**
Honors **PAC-10 record in scoring, rebounds, and blocks; National Player of the Year (1994); All-American (1993, 1994); WNBA MVP (2001)**

★ CAREER HIGHLIGHTS ★

- Lisa played 60 games in 1995–96. That included eight Olympic games and 49 games on the team's world tour.

- Lisa led the WNBA in rebounds in 1997 and 1998.

- Lisa has led her team to two WNBA titles. Both times, she has been named the Championship MVP.

- In 2002, Lisa became the first WNBA player to reach 3,000 points.

★ ★ ★

ABOUT THE AUTHOR

Mark Stewart grew up in New York City in the 1960s and 1970s—when the Mets, Jets, and Knicks all had championship teams. As a child, Mark read everything about sports he could lay his hands on. Today, he is one of the busiest sportswriters around. Since 1990, he has written close to 500 sports stories for kids, including profiles on more than 200 athletes, past and present. A graduate of Duke University, Mark served as senior editor of *Racquet,* a national tennis magazine, and was managing editor of *Super News,* a sporting goods industry newspaper. He is the author of Grolier's All-Pro Biography series and eight titles in the Children's Press Sports Stars series.